A Dog *and* *a* Quest

Godfrey Garner

ISBN 979-8-88540-853-0 (paperback)
ISBN 979-8-88540-854-7 (digital)

Christian Faith Publishing
832 Park Avenue
Meadville, PA 16335
www.christianfaithpublishing.com

Printed in the United States of America

Preface

I just had to sit there, having peed on every object within dog sight and smell, worthy of being peed upon, and reflect on the things that brought me and my human to this time and this place. Looking around the mountains and hills of the Northern Arizona Navajo reservation, I felt a bit disoriented. I also felt a sense of awe at the spectacular beauty God had prepared for us mere dogs. Yep, dogs can feel humility and appreciation for the world's beauty, and we also know that the same God who provided that beauty to our *humans* also provided the gift of *us dogs* to our humans. The reason he did this is because of pure love for the human, and for us dogs. We understand that.

Navajo Nation first responders. Their ancestors were also among the *first Americans*, and their recent generation fought and died protecting it from formidable enemies in WWII. They have a profound love for God and for our great country.

Us dogs are said by the *smarter* of the human population, to have the *tenacity of a lion* coupled with the *love of a sheep for the shepherd*, so naturally, we understand the love between Jesus and our human.

Other than this, the main thing you need to know for the moment is that only a few of us can write, and among those few, fewer still can write like me, *Tom Dooley*. Yep, that's my name, *Tom Dooley*.

As a matter of fact, while we're on the subject, I guess I should explain a couple of additional things about me. I am pretty smart. Note, I didn't say obedient; I said smart. Being obedient, as a matter of fact, is sometimes synonymous (Note the use of that word *synonymous*. Not all dogs can just open their mouths and have something so eloquent—there you have it again, eloquent—simply roll off their tongues.) with being sort of "dull." It often takes a stroke of genius to respond to your human, when he tosses that ball. *You know, there may be a plausible reason for you wanting me to go put that nasty thing in my mouth and bring it back to you, right after you've thrown it away, but at the moment I can't see it. Therefore, I'm gonna pass on the chasing the ball thing for the time being while I contemplate more important things, like writing this book.*

So expanding on that theme, I am, in all humility, really really smart, verging on *greatness*. Thus the moniker, Tom Dooley, the *Great* Pyrenees…get it? So now you know why it's a better idea for *me* to write this book.

My human (though he is a fairly good writer on his own) wanted to have a dog's perspective on the search for the elusive, God-fearing, God-loving, America-loving, military-loving, police-loving, silent majority out there (we'll get to that momentarily). Besides, everyone knows a slight discreet sniff of our human's butt (or anyone's butt as far as that goes), and we dogs can write a book, or at least a kick-ass short story about said individual, bringing back generations past and talents once thought lost. Everyone knows that from as far back as the Holmesian-like bloodhounds of days gone by, that simple whiff (though difficult to handle at times) of our human's butts can tell us where he walked in the past twenty-four hours, how he slept the night before, and often, even what he dreamed about.

And that brings me to our search and to *beautiful* Northern Arizona. Actually, you see, we are, as I take pen to paper, on a quest—on an adventure of sorts—in search of that something my human thinks has been lost. I say *my human thinks* because I don't believe it's lost at all, and I'm here to find it and prove to him that it was never lost in the first place.

Again, the *it* of which I speak is that individual American, love of God, and country. The conservative patriotic love of country that has called young men for generations to stand up for our nation and our way of life, even when that *standing up* has caused some to lose their lives.

Again, to understand this venture better, remember one thing most humans lose sight of when they're rubbing our bells and grabbing us by our floppy ears and giving us a good shake, and that is, us dogs all love God, and we're all patriots. Matter of fact, I don't know one dog from our neighborhood back in Edwards, Mississippi, that ain't a true God-fearing American patriot.

Even those snooty European breeds like that really stuck-up French poodle down the street, Amazing Grace. "Amazing," hummpph. The only thing amazing about her is that she doesn't trip over her own feet 'cause her nose is always so high in the air. She can't possibly see where she's walking, and the only scents she gets to those nostrils come from the birds and insects that fly by.

Yep, even Grace barks and howls along with the rest of us when our neighbor Raphael sings along with the *National Anthem* playing on the radio in his window at the beginning of baseball games on Saturday and Sunday, as he's daydreaming of his opera-singing days. And you wouldn't be able to avoid the chills up your spine when my best friend, Trump, the German shepherd, lips slightly trembling, a small tear trailing slowly down from his right eye, responds to the sounds of that wonderful rendition of, *Oh, say can you see.*

My best German friend, *Trump*.

Yep, all dogs go to heaven (Of course, there's animals in heaven. Remember that verse about the lion laying down with the lamb—not sure I believe that though.), and all dogs love God and America and their *human* in that order. The question is, *do all humans* love in the same order and intensity? I personally think so, and I'm here to prove it to my human, which brings me to him, Poppy.

Me and my human on Patrick AFB, Florida. We go
everywhere together. I usually stay in the truck though when
he's out pumping gas, so I can answer the phone. 'Course,
if I don't recognize the number, I ain't answering.

The Elusive *It* for Which We Search

My human (I call him Poppy. He got that name from the kids
in the neighborhood. Most of them are too young to pronounce his
real name, Godfrey, hence, Poppy.) has often talked about the loss of

that all-encompassing *love* for *everything* America. It took me some time to realize exactly what he was talking about, but when it hit me, it was perfectly simple. And just like everything else, one finally understands (once such *understanding* sweeps over you), it carries with it a warmth of inclusion—the type of inclusion that comes with that simple knowledge of something, everyone else has known for some time. It's like there's a club consisting of everyone who *knows* something. Once you finally know/understand it, you are, from that time forward, a member in good standing.

Poppy tries hard to talk to me, and I love him for it. Sometimes he uses some sorta sign language to tell me things, hands flying all around the place like I'm one of those Egyptian dogs or something. He forgets at times that Thomas Dooley is a *great*—not a *good*—but a *great* Pyrenees. Usually, I *know* what he's telling me. 'Course, I guess most humans do that, the *flyin' hands thingy*.

That said, we dogs don't actually talk to even each other. However, we do long to do that though…to talk to each other, I mean. Funny thing though, we never quite realize that we've been doing it all along…kinda like talking to God I guess. We make the *simple*, complicated and can never actually accept it when it happens.

You seem surprised. Dogs can philosophize too.

So once I understood the issue and was finally a *member in good standing*, I had the ability and the *right* to argue with him as to whether *it* (God-fearing, America-loving America) was still with us or was out there somewhere, just waiting to be found/rediscovered.

As I said, I was of the opinion that it had always been with us and was in fact right around the corner in our own backyard. 'Course, the folks I hung around with, ol' Snot-a-lot and Lupie Lopez and even snooty ol' Amazing Grace were red, white, and blue, right down to their toenails. So obviously, I was of the opinion that Poppy was just getting a little old and maybe pine for the ol' days when humans did funny things like sitting on the front porch, waving American flags when the parade went by.

"You see, my friend, Dooley," he said one day as he looked long-ingly at the distant hills instead of me (Poppy had a habit of saying things like, *my friend* and *you see*, when he was going to say something he saw as profound and was directing it toward me, with the assumption that I didn't know what he was talking about, so he could say most anything and see it as profound, when all the while, you my readers, my friends, know that, *I understood it perfectly*), "in order for an individual to have a deep love for anything, especially something like their home, their country, they have to have sacrificed something for it. They have to have paid something for it, and the more they've paid, the more they love it."

Sometimes Poppy is like a child; he needs to see new and exciting things, things he is absolutely sure lay just over the horizon. 'Course, dogs are like that too, I guess.

When he gets these melancholy feelings, he comes to me and strokes my head 'cause he knows I care, and I'm always there for him. He also does this when he's sad. He does it because I'm soft. All humans, from babies to adults, crave the touch of *soft*. They get comfort from soft things. That's why they carry teddy bears long after they should have discarded them.

Oh well, back to the story. Here, he redirected his gaze toward me and gently waved an *instructional finger*, as he lowered his voice and spoke slowly, clearly, and distinctly, while I cocked my head to one side and growled in a low serious tone, embracing the profundity, which I was confident would soon usher forth from his mouth, "Our leaders, in their infinite wisdom, have seen fit to remove the necessity of anyone, having to sacrifice anything, for their country. It's just free to them. And since its "free", its value to those who don't have to sacrifice is *proportionate*."

I growled low in acquiescence, though this time, I had no idea what he had just said.

He lowered his voice once more, lowered his gaze, staring a hole through the floor below him, and spoke somberly, "To these who are given everything and sacrifice nothing, their nation holds no value whatsoever."

Damn, that sounded important.

Suddenly, another thought struck him, and his demeanor became animated like a kid on the front row of class, who is struck by a lightning bolt having realized the correct answer to a math problem that has heretofore perplexed the class.

He sat bolt upright in his chair and waved his *formerly calm instructional finger* excitedly in my face. I must admit, his excitement was contagious as it often is for me, and I responded with two short sharp barks.

"And guess what happens at this point, my friend," he continued distinctly and slowly, as one with the confidence of he *who knows*, "these folks who've received *all* and sacrificed nothing, begin to look around them, at those who actually did *pay*, for what *they* got for free, and they begin to feel a slight disgust with themselves—a very disturbing feeling of self-loathing that is amplified when they see a veteran with one leg or a grave of one brave soldier who *gave all*. Then soon, that bit of self-loathing morphs slowly into self-hate, and since it is rare for a human being to *hate himself* or to take the responsibility for failing to *step up to the plate*, they begin to hate those who did."

Here, he paused for a moment in search of the right words. "They don't hate them for sacrificing, mind you," he added, waving that ol' instructional finger slowly back and forth, "but for reminding them that *they* didn't. It's sort of like that sense of conviction a sinner gets when he's having to sit beside a repentant person. It hurts for a bit, and humans have an instinct to lash out at someone or something that causes them to hurt."

"Soooo," he continued in summation, easing back into his chair, "we come full circle. Those who receive something they didn't have to pay for, value it at about the same level as that they paid for it, and they tend to despise those, who by virtue of their simple appearance, remind them that they are," here he searched for a moment then spread his hands wide in an *aha* moment, "freeloaders."

Now there's another thing you may want to consider about Poppy, a couple of things as a matter of fact, that would help you see things from his perspective. Poppy fought in two wars. He was a veteran of the war in Vietnam, and because of a long lapse in service, also did two tours in Afghanistan with the 20th Special Forces

Group. A background like that just sort of primes one for loving the nation for which he fights.

"You know what, my friend," he'd often chuckle to himself, while he scratched me under the chin (a good attentive human always knows just where to scratch under the chin to get an idle tail wagging like it's wound up), "you never really know just how much you love the good Lord, until you hear the high-pitched whine of bullets whizzing by your ear, and it suddenly occurs to you that the only thing that keeps one of those things from splitting your skull is that very same *good Lord*."

"Yep," he'd often continue, "the more you hear that sound and realize that you're still alive when the music stops, the more you happen to love that same Lord and Savior."

"The leap from *God-lovin'* to *America-lovin'* is easy to fathom since you realize that God is keeping you alive and safe so you can defend *America*," he continued, "and you have to love that very same *America* and all the folks in it, in order to risk your very life to defend it. Once you've made that connection, the inclusion of *all* police officers and first responders is an easy step."

"You see, Dooley," he'd always add, as if to clear up any misunderstanding he was sure I might be harboring, "it's just natural to love God and America, and by extension, all those folks who risk life and limb to protect her and to acknowledge the God who gave her to us. It's just amazing to me that anyone would lose that love for her."

"It's even more amazing to me that someone would not only lose the love for her, but actually criticize her and criticize those who fight for her," he'd usually add, with increasing anger and frustration.

"I mean, why would someone speak out against their own home, and at the same time, not have the courage to just leave and go live somewhere else?"

At this point, he'd begin the arguing mode, "No, Thomas Dooley, I know you think that love for God and country is still alive and well, and I'd love to agree with you, but I just can't see it. It's gone the way of the dinosaur or the eight-track."

The Quest: A Living Thing

I know this sounds odd to the skeptics out there, but Poppy and I have an understanding of sorts. I want my devoted followers and readers to understand me and to understand him. We've been together for so long that, not unlike other dogs and humans out there, we can actually understand each other to a degree. 'Course, maybe it's just a realization that we sort of agree on certain things without actually understanding the essence, sorta like the best topping for strawberry ice cream.

Either way, it's good for us because most of my friends aren't very easy to talk to, and besides, they don't spend a lot of time mulling over ideas like Poppy and I do. And as for him, he doesn't have a lot of friends who care to listen to him very intently, and as it is that I can't talk in that way or interject, other than a short low growl or high-pitched yap now and then, I do a lot of listening. Occasionally, those little ideas just sort of seep through, hit something deep inside me and come careening off back to him.

Such is the process when he finally accepted the fact that maybe I was right, and maybe the America he longed so for was still out there. Once he caught on to that idea, then accepted the fact that all we had to do was go on a road trip (with which we closely identified), things took on a life of their own, and the ubiquitous "snowball" started rolling downhill and gaining speed along the way. As it did so, he passed along little tidbits reference the *quest*.

"You see," he'd offer occasionally as he made another one of the constant lists of things that must be carried along the way, "a *quest* is like a living thing. It takes on a life of its own, much like a living entity. It breathes, it coughs occasionally, it slows then gains speed, and it is in a constant state of energetic stress waiting patiently like a horse, straining at the reins anxious, to spring forward."

As this interchange was in the form of a symbiotic relationship, I would occasionally offer little tidbits about the canine world, with which Poppy, knowledgeable as he was, was unfamiliar.

For instance, he once got involved in a little scrape among a couple of the neighborhood dogs, trying hard to assure neither one hurt the other. For his efforts, he received a couple of bites and scratches. For the rest of the day, he opined that the dogs in question were somehow mad at him for intervening. This disturbed him since he prided himself in his relationship with the neighborhood pets.

I had to explain, and it was no easy task I assure you, that dogs don't get mad at humans, even if they are *humans* belonging to someone else. They just *don't*. Anger at a human, in such a fashion, is simply unknown among dogs. Even dogs that have never laid eyes on a particular human will try extremely hard to tie themselves emotionally to any human who pays the least bit of attention to them. We just love our humans in such a manner, and expect that same level of love in return, which is unfortunately missing on occasion.

The knowledge of basics of the *quest*, however, was extremely important to me. Breathing life into it from the beginning was going to make it much more personal for me, and I was anxious to get started, which we were closer and closer to doing.

The Humans Chosen for Us

You know, as strange as it is that a *dog writer* like me would find himself on a mountain on the Navajo reservation in Northern Arizona, the humans we dogs find ourselves with is stranger still. We dogs have always loved talking about our humans to the other dogs in the neighborhood. Yep, we love our humans, but you gotta admit, some of them are pretty hard to housebreak, and teaching them how to fetch a stick is a real challenge.

As I said, my name is Tom Dooley, and I am a Great Pyrenees. Again, not just *good* mind ya, *great*. It's important that you remember this. Poppy told me the story of the name Tom Dooley, something about some guy hanging from a tall oak tree for some reason that I could never fathom. 'Course that's understandable 'cause after all, I am still a *dog*. He also told me that Clark Gable (no, I'm not sure who he is either) played a lead role in the very last movie of his career alongside Marilyn Monroe (happened to also be the very last movie of her career as well). They both died after starring in *The Misfits*, and in that movie, Clark Gable had a dog named Tom Dooley, and Poppy thought it was a cool name. For a while, I was afraid my name was going to be *dammit* 'cause Poppy kept yelling, "Come here, *dammit*," when he was trying to teach me stuff (all that yellin', just because I stuck my nose in the toilet one day; still haven't figured that one out). Never cared much for the name *dammit*, so all in all, *Tom Dooley* sounded pretty good.

Anyhow, back to me and my relationship with Poppy. For some reason, known only to God, fate had decreed that I should, early on, wind up in the hands of a *vagabond* human. A vagabond, of course, is a human doomed to wander the earth searching for something he can't identify, always searching, the kind of never-ending search that is a constant tug on the heart. As such, he'll never find it, and he will continue to wander the earth, searching.

I love the ol' guy, but he's also one of those Vietnam vets, and as a general rule (some of my buddies own *Vietnam vet-humans*, and in the neighborhood, we have a tendency to talk about them), they have a hard time realizing anyone or anything can love them. Matter of fact, he once told me that the only three things humans needed to be happy were something to do, something to look forward to, and somebody to love.

Now luckily, Poppy vagabond, Poppy also has a house, two as a matter of fact, so we are allowed to stop now and then for respite from the road. Actually, all in all, I didn't then and I don't now, mind being attached to a vagabond once I learned the ropes. Yeah, of course, I vomited in the truck once in a while when I first learned about the road, but soon I got my "truck legs" so to speak, and I began to enjoy it. I had no idea how many odors would pass by your nose while you had your head hanging out the window. You have to be quick to absorb them all, and of course, that's impossible. All in all, it's a great life, and I love hanging out with him on the road.

Poppy takes me everywhere with him. Sometimes we stay in nice hotel rooms. Sometimes we stay with friends, and sometimes we just ride all night, listening to the wind whistle by outside. He likes to tell me stories about how things must have been for folks back in the old days before plastic bones and other stuff to chew on.

Once I convinced him to go on this quest, all we had to do was a little planning. The actual traveling part, we'd gotten used to years before. He's getting a little old, in human years, and I think this might be his/our last book, *A Dog and a Quest.* All in all, it sounds neat.

Chapter 1

Understanding Me/ Understanding Him

Poppy wanted me to tell the story, and once I understood *what and how*, it just seemed like a perfect idea. There were, of course, some glitches that had to be worked out. Dogs don't normally write books, but we crossed each *glitch* as it came to us, and soon we had a routine. Poppy is not only a hell of a neat guy, he's also pretty smart, and even though he doesn't realize it, he's a pretty damn good writer. He talks to me a lot. 'Course, there's no one else around for him to talk to, so it makes sense.

I overheard him once commenting to himself that he was completely independent and didn't need anyone. I think male humans like to see themselves that way. 'Course, the down side of that, for a human, is that it occasionally means *no one wants to have anything to do with you, often because you have a tendency to be an asshole.*

Lately, he's lamented the loss of *his* America. *His* America, I understand, is the home he grew up in where everyone loved the Lord and the country and our military and our police officers and firemen.

I really love Poppy and wouldn't want my life any other way. I think he loves me too. He hugs me really tight once in a while, and I can almost hear or see him sort of weeping a little. I have learned that male humans aren't supposed to do that, so he probably just figures he's safe with me, and of course, he is.

We've grown to be able to communicate pretty well. That's a good thing too, in light of this book. He says it's his last, but he's said that before. The funny thing is, most of the time, he just rattles away, not thinking I can understand what he's saying. We get the messages back and forth though, and me being the one to tell this story, our ability to communicate has been helped along a great deal. It's funny…sometimes, I almost think I can hear a bark or two coming from him.

Us

Now if I'm going to be successful telling this story, and you're going to be successful understanding it, I gotta explain a few more things about *me*. 'Course, it's not *me*; it's more like *us*, and the *us* I speak of in this sense is *us dogs*.

You see, dogs can talk. Well, not talk in the way you humans mean, but more like *communicate*, I guess. And this is important because most people don't think we can do that. As dogs, if we could actually talk, I'd tell you flat out, we do not read minds. Folks who really love dogs (and God bless 'em) like to propose that concept (*my dog actually knows what I'm thinking before I say it…yadayadayada*), but the fact is, it ain't so.

I say that to explain this, *and this is important*; as I said before, Poppy is not only a vagabond; he's a writer. He doesn't think he's as good as he is, but he enjoys doing it, and I like to encourage him. So I cock my head now and then when he's sitting at the computer and reading something he's just written to me. Again, I do that to encourage him 'cause I know it makes him happy. And because he's good at it, I am pretty sure I can be good at it too. I've watched him do it enough times.

Then there's the fact that dogs have egos just like humans, and I always get a kick outta hearing him read my name from the pages of one of his books. He always shows it to me too, even though he must know that I can't read either.

From the time I was just a puppy, he always liked to talk to me too, even though he knew back in the early days, I had absolutely no idea what he was saying. I don't now, and didn't then, see a problem with it (not being able to understand what he's saying), but since day 1, I've sort of realized that he's much happier if I "seem to understand him." So now and then, I cock my head one way or the other, you know…like I understand perfectly what he just said, and he always gets a kick out of it.

Okay, back to the issue of *communication*. Now, while it's true what they say that some among us dogs are what you might call "people whisperers," and are thought to be able to understand every word a human speaks, I personally can't attest to that. I just never met one, a real "people whisperer." Besides, to tell you the truth, I don't see the value in that. I've learned to understand almost everything I need to. You just gotta appreciate the difference between *words* and *sounds*.

The problem, of course, lies there, in the difference between *actual words* and *sounds*. Now *words* are simple and bland. Often, they don't even have any *music* to them. They're just blah, blah, blah, unless of course Poppy is trying to point out that I just tracked a blob of mud into the house or something like that, but even then, the words are still just words, loud words, but *words* still. A few *dammits* mixed in here and there for a sort of musical-like emphasis, but even then, they're still just words.

Sounds, on the other hand, can ordinarily tell you a lot of things. I usually try to convey a whole bucket of thought in my early morning *bark* (usually around 5:00 a.m.), when Poppy first lets me out of the house. I try my best to tell the whole gang that I'm up, and they should be too, because after all, it's 5:00 a.m., and the sun will soon rise "to greet me." There's a whole bunch of sounds in that, and they can all be conveyed with a really good, loud, throaty bark. Greatest sound in the world. *Words*, they just can't compare. Sorry.

Some of my buddies try to convey the same thoughts through a low rumbling growl, but I just never got into that. One of my ol' blunt-nosed bulldog buddies from the neighborhood, Sir Snot-a-Lot once told me that really intense growling took a lot of effort, and you can easily get your upper lip tangled in your teeth. Just couldn't see the benefit in it.

Another example of good communication with just a little movement for instance, when we're riding in the front seat of the truck with our humans, and we reach out with our paws, extend our claws ever so slightly (some of you humans have really sensitive skin), and tug a little at their forearm. All we're saying is, "I just want a little kiss on the nose. That's all I need, then you can go back to turning that wheelie thing around." Now how can *words* get any better than that, I ask ya. If only humans could learn a few good barks.

This is *my* chair and you know it.

Day One

The first day for a dog and their *human* is probably the most important day in a dog's life. I can safely say, it's more important than the day they come "diving" out of their mama. (I overheard my doctor, Dr. Lena Jo, the most beautiful dog doctor in the world, tell Poppy that dogs always put their little paws under their chin and actually come "diving" out of their mama, as if they can't wait to greet the world.)

Yep, the difference between you and me is, I make this look *good.*

On my first day home, he made the mistake of placing me in this really soft chair. I just sort of figured it was *mine* from that time on. He didn't know how to "properly" use it anyhow. A couple of funny things happened that first day. 'Course, I realized the moment we met that Poppy—well, I hesitate to say this, but the simple fact is, he *needed* me. That chair, ahhhh, not so much; he didn't *need* that. Especially after I peed on it, sorta claiming it, in the traditional sense, you know. Yeah, he didn't need that chair. *Me*, on the other hand, *without a doubt...*he needed.

In actuality, that first day also had an earlier beginning. I guess you could say, it was our first day in our house, a house we would share for years to come—*years* in the dog, as well as human sense. It all began much earlier than that however. You see, our house is in Mississippi, but (I don't brag about this much because I think it kinda *stings* Poppy a little) I happen to be a *Texas* dog.

My real mama, the lady who rescued me from a buncha yapping brothers and sisters and held me for Poppy (he happened to be in Afghanistan at the time, and she had promised him that she would find me, rescue me, and hold me for his return) happens to live around San Antonio. I remember the day she picked me up. I heard her later comment that she knew I was the one because when she first laid eyes on me, even though you couldn't tell any difference between me and all my brothers and sisters, I happened to have my nose stuck under the tail of one of the females in the litter. Somehow, my mama figured that was a sign that Poppy and I were destined to *be*. I have no idea why.

Yeah, all that's true, but I'm also "mean and vicious," so watch it.

Sense of Humor

Sense of humor, yeah, all dogs have them. We love practical jokes too. Like that damn little *yappie* Mexican dog down the street, Lupie Lopez, who always farts just when one of the guys sniffs his butt, then laughs this high, irritating, squeaky laugh like he just thought it up. Hell, he's been doing it since I've known him. The guys all know about it, but we hide and wait when a new dog comes in the neighborhood. It is kinda funny in a way.

Humans don't know this, but among dogs, that is definitely bad manners. Kinda like humans picking their noses right before they shake hands with you, but with Lupie, it's understandable. You'd know that if you ever saw his human. Big, fat-assed woman who always wears shorts that bunch up around her crotch. Nobody sniffs her ass, I can tell ya that for sure.

Dogs are influenced a lot by their humans when it should be the other way around. Like for instance, humans are attracted to each other because of the way they look or smile or wear their hair or something. I know this because every now and then, when we're just driving around, Poppy will say something like, "Damn, Tom Dooley (He never uses both my names unless I peed on the floor or he is really impressed by some girl's butt. I know this because of the way he usually finishes that *damn Tom Dooley* sentence.), have you ever seen such a beautiful butt in all your born days." I'm still not sure what a *butt* is, though I usually bark enthusiastically, as if I knew exactly what he was talking about. This seems to please him.

As far as influencing me, this has encouraged me to search for that particular part of the body, in my friends in the neighborhood. None of my friends knows what it is either. I'm trying to teach him the value of a discreet sniff though. Yep, humans would be much better off if they allowed their dogs to influence them a bit more… and if they sniffed each other's butts when they first met.

Chapter 2

Parting

Dogs understand from their humans that there is something somewhat daunting about separating yourself from the familiar, especially if your destination lies somewhere among the *totally unfamiliar*. This *unfamiliarity* and the daunting emotions it portends for humans is felt most acutely among the elderly humans, but it is also felt in the extreme among all ages of canines. You see, dogs become attached, quickly and tightly, to their first home and its surroundings, and leaving it for any extended time is threatening to them. When they have to leave, they get anxious and *homesick*. I always felt this, but I handled it by tucking my nose and legs back under my body, sorta like my friend turtle.

A little more attention from their humans can solve the problem though, like a few strokes under the chin or something. Dogs suffer from attention deficit disorder (ADD) too, just like humans. Only "doggie style" means not getting enough attention.

Yep, dogs bond quickly and tightly, with their territorial surroundings and are quick to defend it from outsiders or intruders. Like I said, being separated from their home is highly stressful for them. As such, I can understand Poppy, in his elderly state, being reluctant to leave while at the same time feeling the "pull of that which lies over the *next ridgeline*." Such is the dichotomy confronting the *vagabond*. It lurks deep within the DNA of Poppy. He can't stay, and he's often afraid to leave. Heck, I understand that.

"There's just something a little fearful about it anymore," he spoke wistfully to me early one morning after we'd decided that there was only one way to solve this puzzle and find that which we thought was lost. "It's almost like the daunting feeling of having to write a novel," he continued.

Now Poppy had written several novels at that time, and each time he'd start one, he'd voice the same laments: "I'll never be able to finish, I don't even know what I'm doing this time, I just don't have it in me anymore."

He always voiced the same fears, but he always finished, and each time, his work was admirable, and he was proud of what he'd accomplished. Each time, he'd do it the way he'd done it the time before: one day at a time, one page at a time, stopping at the end of the last sentence on that page, and vowing not to take up the pen again until the following day. Each time, it worked.

"With this trip though"—he patted me gently on the head—"I just feel lonely. I feel like I'm thrusting myself somewhere I have no business going, somewhere I do not belong. They belong here." He waved a finger haphazardly across the distant horizon at unseen "theys." "They've worked to earn the right to belong, but it took them a long time. I just don't have that much time left."

Because I understand him and how he felt, and because I understand the need he had to take the show on the road in search of the elusive *deeply God-fearing conservative American* just to prove he has not succumbed to extinction, I took the responsibility to make this quest mine, insisting that he come along to assist me in "telling this tale."

Besides, every dog knows, if you eat Blue Bell coffee ice cream with peanut butter on it, and you always remember to forgive yourself, everything will work out okay in the long run.

Another thing factored in here: this trip took place sometime shortly after the beginning of COVID-19, the China Flu. It was, however, a great time for dogs then. People had finally come to the realization that *dog kisses* were not the grossest things a person could be exposed to. Matter of fact, I think a lot of folks kinda got the idea that some good ol' *dog snot* might just cure ya of things, sort of like "posies in the pocket" back in the age of the Black Death.

The *age*, however, was another reason for humans to be a little apprehensive. I knew, however, that two things, once bound together, the *book* and the *road*, would form a duo he could not resist. And since he loved me and knew that I wanted to do this, he'd have no other alternative than to suppress his apprehension in leaving the familiar and jumping headlong into it. I also knew that once we hit the road and smelled the smells of the unfamiliar and felt the "winds" of change and new environs, he'd soon forget about his comfortable recliner, at least for a few days, and settle into the journey.

In doing this for him, I was doing it for me, and as it turned out, we were doing it for each other. In the end, as you, the reader, will see a *hell of an adventure* unfolded. Even so, I too had a sad parting from my friends. They had a difficult time understanding what I was doing, and to tell you the truth, so did I.

"Why don't you just stay with us, Tom Dooley? We can walk around the ol' neighborhood like we do every day, just sniffin' butts and peeing on stuff. It just ain't gonna be the same around here with you gone, and besides, this thing you're looking for, it's a *human* thing. You shouldn't have to go lookin' for it. Your human should do that," my best buddy, Trump, said between peeing and sniffin' around on my last morning before the trip in the old neighborhood on our daily walk.

Trump is not only my best friend, he's also the smartest dog in town. Why, he will lay down perfectly still just because his human, Dr. Lena Jo, told him to, and he never gets too far away from her when they go walking. Yep, *one of a kind best buddy*. The only thing though, is he just hasn't been able to get the idea of my hunt, my quest, for God-fearing conservative America.

When he says that though, he's got it completely wrong. We dogs do need to find that part of us all, just as much as humans do, 'cause the same God who loves humans loves us dogs too. The same police who loves and protects humans, loves and protects us dogs too (and besides, there's some really tough *nose dogs*, we call 'em, who protect those police officers too). And finally, those soldiers who protect all of America against our enemies, protect us dogs too (and Trump forgets it, but some of his closest brothers, those Germans, also serve right alongside the soldiers). So the America I'm gonna find is not only out there, it's *our* America too…woof, woof (that translates loosely "hell, yeah").

And finally, I sort of blush a little when I say this, but I'm really gonna miss my girlfriend, Myia, next door. She just plain rocks my little "doggie" boat. I'm really gonna miss her.

Chapter 3

The Perfect Chariot for the Perfect Quest

When we finally decided to launch out on this quest, and it was determined that I would tell the story, we also decided that *I* would make most of the decisions on where to go and who to talk to while there. Obviously, however, Poppy had to make numerous suggestions just to sort of "prime the pump," I suppose you'd say. After all, I am still just a dog.

"Okay, Tom," he began the period of pump priming early one morning, "the usual first step in planning a trip such as this is to consult a map…you know…a sort of bird's eye view of where you are and where you may want to be after a few days."

Now I quickly realized that a map has a tendency to "hold you." A map sends the message that *you are here, and you'll follow this track until you find yourself here.* The whole process seemed to me to be somewhat confining. I had sort of envisioned us going down this road until we saw another one that seemed to lead us to a more interesting place, even if that wasn't actually the case in the end. Maps were just a little confining.

When I had somehow gotten this message across to Poppy, he simply looked down the road in front of us, looked down at his feet, pointed at the ground, and said, "We are here," then pointing at the horizon in front of him. "With a little effort and the good Lord willing, one day soon, we will be there. Along the way, we'll talk to folks in a sincere effort to locate that elusive creature we seek."

He also suggested we follow a generally westward track and stick fairly close to a road, euphemistically referred to as Route 66. He did have a loosely organized reason for Route 66 and for the general westward direction. "You see, Tom"—he smiled as one would at a knowledge-seeking youth—"folks in search of anything throughout history, whether it be knowledge or adventure or opportunity, have always moved west to find it. Makes perfect sense, therefore, this is the direction we should take."

As I had no reason whatsoever to argue this point with him, I simply looked west and barked loudly, sniffing at the air somewhere above my head for "I know not what," and we were off.

I love Poppy for a lot of reasons, probably most important, he loves me. I don't think he meant to get too attached to a dog at first, but he told me once that he'd had so many people in his life in the past, who just hadn't, for one reason or another, stuck around, he just figured I wouldn't either. But he didn't know that dogs don't leave humans; humans leave dogs. I wasn't gonna go anywhere, and once he and I started going everywhere together, it just became clear that we were meant for each other, and neither of us were gonna go anywhere. And this trip was going to be the best ever. We were on a quest.

Now it took me some time to understand what a quest was, but I finally figured out it was like searching for that perfect bone, the one you buried last summer, the one that fit your back teeth just perfectly; the one you could chew forever and it never got any smaller or broke off and got stuck between your teeth. Yeah…the one you had no idea where you buried.

We were going out in search of that all elusive metaphoric "bone." Poppy told me that it was a bone that America had once owned collectively, and though we hadn't buried it, we had somehow misplaced it.

I guess it could be described as a shared feeling or a commitment. It wasn't even a thing; it was a *time* and a corresponding *feeling*. It was a shared love for something real but something that couldn't be described. Poppy told me once it was like a *smell*, a smell that everyone recognized, but no two people in the entire country could describe it to each other and get it right.

Well, I knew right off the bat what it was. It was sorta like Lupie Lopez's human crotch; even though every dog in the neighborhood knew what it smelled like, no one could describe it.

"There was a time once," he told me, "when all of America got a tear in their eyes listening to 'The Star-Spangled Banner' being sung by someone with a beautiful voice, and a family member who'd never returned from Vietnam or Korea, when people wore their best shoes to church and everyone went to church on Sunday."

"It was a time when people of every color and ethnicity respected the guy in a uniform with a badge on his chest," he continued, "and I'm just afraid it's gone for good."

The decision that I should write about it just came naturally. It also made a lot of sense. Yep, he and I decided early on that I was going to have to commemorate the trip in a book. This story was going to have to be mine. Only I could write it because I had no idea what he was talking about. If I found it and described it, therefore, it pretty much had to be real. He wanted to find it so bad, he just might fudge a little bit…being a dog, I had no idea what a "fudge" was or how to do it.

Now I know the idea of a dog writing a book is a little foreign to most folks. Kids can accept it, but adults are just a little more skeptical, I guess you'd say. Why, I'll bet there ain't ten grown-ups in the country who could tell you the name of the last dog who won the coveted Puplitzer prize for literature—shameful. I may not be the best writer in the world, but I've been watching Poppy and listening to him read parts of his books back to me, and I think I got it. Either way, I'm gonna give it a shot.

Like all adventures, we just started out sort of daydreaming and asking that famed question, "What if we…yadayadayada," and it just rolled from there. The real key to it was to get the perfect ride or "chariot," as Poppy calls it. Poppy told me that vagabonds of old just took off down the road with a little rolled up handkerchief on a stick slung across their shoulder. He told me he never had been able to figure out what they carried in the rolled-up handkerchief, but if you were a true "vagabond," you had to carry one.

We were the new breed of vagabond. We covered a lot more territory, so naturally we had to have the perfect ride. It had to be perfect 'cause we wanted folks to *want* to look at it. Any ol' weenie dog can ride down the road with his head hanging out the window of a Ford Escort, ears flopping around in the wind, happily sucking the stuck bugs out of his teeth, but we were gonna go in style.

We started out looking for the perfect ol' van (Poppy called it a "hippie" van), on the exterior of which we would paint pictures of… *me*, what else. Then we realized that it was gonna be a little costly and take a lot of time to fix up, especially since Poppy often got confused about which end of the screwdriver he should use.

We did a lot of praying about it. That's another reason I love Poppy. He's always willing to admit that he needs to rely on the good Lord when he's trying to figure out which end of the screwdriver to use. Yep, he prays a lot, and most of the time, he's on his knees by the bed. I love to see him do that 'cause I can sneak up and stick my nose underneath his chin and nuzzle him. Scared him at first, but he expects it now.

Poppy took a lot of time telling me of the importance of the "perfect chariot." As is the case most of the time he explains something to me, he was more than likely trying to explain it to himself. It got a little complicated, until one day he just said to me/himself, "You know what, Thomas Dooley (he used the formal in those times when he's struck by an epiphany…a little softer than a rock, I think, its sorta like a period at the end of a really long sentence that never actually goes anywhere, and it usually means there's no reason to dwell on the subject anymore, I think), we're spending too much time thinking about it…let's just do it, say a prayer, and all the pieces will fall perfectly into the place they were intended to land, not a doubt in my/our mind right, Thomas?"

That very day, God just answered his prayers and sent his good friend and Masonic brother Jim Stillwell to him. You see, Jim had an itching to go on a road trip, and just so happened to have a forty feet travel coach that needed to be driven. All we had to do then was paint *me* on the sides of it in a paint we could take off later, and we were ready to hit the road.

That simple prayer, just like all simple prayers, was answered in a way only God can do, and launched the creation of the most beautiful chariot that ever cruised the sacred pavement of Route 66 from Northeast Oklahoma, to the fertile (if somewhat tarnished of late) rolling hills and plains of John Steinbeck. 'Course I loved it because it had pictures of me all over it. Now what the heck is there *not to like* about that?

Not to put too *fine a point* on it.

The real story of my van, however, starts from the beginning, as it of course should. Poppy told me about a van he owned and even lived in, off and on, in leaner times and in between marriages (humans have a tendency to connect with each other for life, over and over again).

Anyhow, this particular van had what he called "character." I'm not sure exactly what that is, but it must have been important to him because he got a whimsical smile on his face whenever he recalled it.

"Yeah," he would say, drawing the word out in a somewhat dreamy fashion, "I packed everything I owned in that van, and I did it one summer afternoon, on the spur of the moment when I'd suddenly decided to change my entire life, including where I lived, by the way." He interjected as though it was the main point of the story.

"You see, Tom," he continued, "I'd finally decided after a few months of having really screwed up my life to that point that I wasn't going to be able to repair the breaks and fissures in the wall, even after numerous sloppy attempts to do so, so I may as well chuck the entire thing and just start over."

"Yep, I was sort of proud of the fact that my entire life to that point, fit nicely into this old Chevy van, which by the way," he was quick to add, "had two twin-size mattresses in the back."

"There's something to be said about traveling light, even if you have no choice in the matter." He chuckled as he recalled.

"I just decided to take Tony, my oldest son and best friend, and…go home."

For Poppy, "home" at that time was the great state of Mississippi. He had, following two tours in Vietnam, gotten married, fathered two beautiful children, settled in Tulsa, Oklahoma, as a police officer, and suddenly made horrendous mistakes: lost his marriage of seventeen years, left his job, remarried following a whirlwind romance, promptly divorced again, woke up one morning totally lost.

BTW, he didn't have me at the moment, which no doubt was another mistake he'd made (us dogs can often soothe the savage beasts, as long as these same beasts ain't us).

"I just figured that a change in, well…everything…was in order," he continued, following a brief moment of reflection.

"That ol' van" somehow transported me to a new start and a place where I could possibly fix a bunch of things I'd broken.

A seemingly long silence ensued, at which time he suddenly snapped his fingers and interjected, "And that's just what we need to make this momentous trip."

Just so there's no confusion.

Our initial plan was to locate a similar old van, with similar "old character" (I still didn't know exactly what that was), fix it up on the inside sorta like the original one, paint the sides to show the world we were looking at, as we drove down the road, what we were carrying on the inside, and just hit the road in search of our quarry.

Such, however, was happily not to be the case. One of Poppy's best friends, Jim Stillwell, happened by one day. Now Jim had been discussing the trip with Poppy, and clearly had an idea of going along. But Jim, also, had a motor coach.

"Godfrey," Jim offered one day out of the blue, "why don't you just take my motor coach. It's plenty big enough and a lot more comfortable than an old van, and besides, it needs to be driven. It's just been sitting out in my front yard for weeks, getting rusty. I could change the oil and have her ready to go in a few days, and if you wanted to, we could even paint the *Tom Dooley* pics on the sides of it, and I'll go along and help with everything."

Poppy and Jim talked about it and talked about it, and the more they talked, the more excited they got. A real life adventure, and they were going to take me along. The trip was going to be great.

I was glad to hear that Poppy's friend, Jim, was going along. Poppy is pretty smart when it comes to telling a story or writing a book, but when it comes to fixing a car or handling the correct end of a screw driver and such, he doesn't know dog poop from peanut butter. Come to think of it, I'm not sure I do either. I suppose it depends on the peanut butter.

They planned and planned and had maintenance done to the motor coach and figured out a route that would take them first to the Tulsa, Oklahoma, area where Poppy could reconnect with some of his old police buddies for a day or so, then on west out Route 66 to search for the all-elusive, dying breed that is God-fearing, conservative America. And finally, the day came.

Throughout the trip, we were supported by our hometown newspaper, *The Clinton Courier*. They reported on our travels to our local supports. (Folks who would have loved to have been with us but were all, for one reason or another, members of the "normal folk." Me and Poppy were by no means, hindered by such restraints as "normality." Anyhow, they, "the normal folk," had the luxury of sitting in front of the TV, beer ensconced firmly in the preferred hand, and read all about our travels in the good ol' Courier.)

We drove first to my veterinarian's clinic so Poppy could say goodbye to his girl, who happened to be my doc, and all of her associates, and we were off. Twenty miles or so, west on Interstate 20 and we were out of Mississippi, heading roughly north by northwest.

Farr Animal Clinic and those we love. Parting is
such sweet…something, something.

Chapter 4

On the Road Again

Guess it goes without saying that a dog doesn't have the opportunity to ride in a motor coach often. I was an ol' pro at riding around in my truck with Poppy. Our regular routine every day was to rise, do what nature required of us, let Poppy grab a to-go cup full of coffee, and jump in the ol' Ford truck to hit the road. I was used to that routine.

We usually drove to Vicksburg, twenty minutes or so down the road, where Poppy would grab a kolache and another cup of coffee (the girls at the doughnut shop always wanted to pet me and talk about how pretty I was when we drove up to the drive-in window, and of course, I didn't mind it much either), and we'd just drive around, window down while we enjoyed the early morning coolness in the air. I would sit comfortably in the front seat with my head hanging out the window, my ears and lips blowing gently in the breeze as Poppy drove. Everything was just the way it was supposed to be.

A strange thing happened though as I boarded that motor coach and we began the trip. Inside the coach, the atmosphere was that of a small living room, not unlike our own house. I stood on a carpet beside a couch and a small kitchen with kitchen counters and a small table to eat meals on. For all seemingly practical purposes, we were in our own house or one similar to it. I just laid down on the soft carpet and began to doze.

All of a sudden, the earth began to move. I hadn't expected the feeling of an ostensibly stable object, rolling down the road, and my feet and legs being unstable underneath me. Took some getting used to, but in the end, it was very pleasant. Right off, I began to hanker to get home and tell Snot-a-Lot about it. Couldn't wait to see the look in his ol' droopy, bloodshot eyes.

We traveled through a good-sized rainstorm for the first couple of hours. The storm seemed to be a sign from heaven that our venture was being blessed. I hadn't seen rain for a long time as it was a pretty dry period for Mississippi. I wanted to run around outside in the cool drops from the sky, as such is in the nature of us dogs. Humans don't seem to understand this. I always laughed at Poppy when he got in the shower and just seemed to relish the drops of water hitting his face and chest, but as soon as a drop or two of rain would hit his face outside, he'd cuss a little and run for cover. Humans are just strange creatures. He does keep me in the house especially when it's really hot outside though, so I don't have to worry about heat much. That's good too because my breed is a hairy one with thick fur.

We finally pulled off the road late in the day in a remote truck parking lot outside Little Rock, Arkansas. Even though I had been lying on the cool carpet on the floor all the way so far, I was tired, as if I'd run a long way. I was used to traveling with Poppy in our truck, but this new chariot just made me tired for some reason. I slept well, as Poppy and his friend did, from the constant snoring.

The morning of the second day, we took off with a positive feeling and a renewed spirit. A new day always renews the spirit, and a short conversation with God, asking him to travel with us, just starts everything off right. Within an hour, we stopped to get gas and check our vehicle, and this is where we ran across our first *God-fearing conservative American.*

His name was Scott, and he was from Florida. He was an over the road trucker and had been driving for twenty years. He had become a Christian about ten years before that and had decided to be a preacher for the truckers, making it his job to tell any of the other truckers about God.

Now I think I talked about this earlier, but it's worth mentioning again 'cause some people just can't seem to grasp the concept. Contrary to belief, we dogs know about God too. We even have our own way of talking to him. It's a lot different from our humans, but we still know him, and we know that he has a little doggie heaven waiting for us as well, when we've taken that last walk with our humans.

What we don't know about though is *preachers*. Sure, Poppy gets dressed every week and goes with his girlfriend (my doctor) somewhere for an hour or so, then comes back and talks about the *preacher* that day and what a good job he did. He never takes me with him though, so I have no idea what the preacher did a *good job* at.

Dogs don't really have anything like preachers. Ol' Snot-a-Lot talks all the time, but most of us don't stand too close to him when he does…all the stuff flyin' all over the place, you know, but I'm not sure whether that's the same thing as preaching.

Well, that day, I finally got to see what a *preacher* looks like and what his name is. Scott told Poppy that he was a preacher and had been for the truckers for ten years. He seemed really excited about it too. Poppy asked him if he was a conservative, and Scott seemed a little astonished at that question.

"Sure, I am," he responded. "How could I be anything else?"

For about fifteen minutes, Scott explained to us what it meant to him to be conservative. In addition to fearing God, and loving the military and our police officers who work so hard to protect us, Scott went on to tell us what it meant to him to be an American and how much he loved this country.

Our first discovery, and it was a good one. I barked a couple of times (my best "I told you so" bark), but I'm not sure Poppy understood me. Felt good though. We dogs do love to show our humans how important it is for them to listen to our advice from time to time. Gonna be a good trip.

Tulsa and the Good Ol' Days

We pulled into the Tulsa area that morning. Poppy had a slight smile on his face as we pulled into the area, and he constantly pointed out various things to Jim as we drove. I realized something I had thought all along but must have forgotten. Humans remember good things a lot more vividly than they remember bad things. Guess that's a way God set things up just 'cause he didn't want his children to be loaded down with a lot of heavy memories and such.

I know Poppy lived and worked here for a long time before he ever met me. He also left, for some reason. If things were as good as he seemed to be remembering right now, there would have been little reason for him to leave, but he did. Seemed he wasn't remembering those *less than good* things now. He pointed things out with a constant smile on his face.

"Okay, Thomas Dooley (he always called me Thomas Dooley when he wanted to emphasize something. If I could laugh, I'd laugh when he did this 'cause it sounded so funny…Thomas Dooley… hahahaha.), in less than an hour, you're going to meet one of my fellow cop brothers, Ron Moulton. Ron and I started out in law enforcement when we were both cops on the security force at Oklahoma University. Man, those were the good ol' days." He smiled, looking off in the distance trying hard to capture some long lost laugh or giddiness, the *giddiness of youth*. "We were constantly broke and constantly optimistic about the dragons we would one day 'slay.'"

"Later"—he turned to me and pointed his finger so as not to lose my attention (this wasn't necessary 'cause dogs are always fixated on their owners. We never even consider diverting our attention to lesser things when our humans are talking directly to us, even though most of the time, we have no clue what they're talking about)—"me and Ron found ourselves working the streets, 'short north' in Tulsa. Man, we had fun back then."

Yep, humans have a tendency to remember the good things about their past and rarely ever center on the bad. Dogs, on the other hand, smell stuff, and good or bad, those smells bring things back. Dogs don't have bad days very often though. Poppy, on the other hand, has a bunch of them. He needs me for such times. I'm glad too.

He went through some bad times in his life, I think. He talks about them now and then, and once in a while when he's with his close friends, I just lay on the floor, snoozing and listening, but mostly listening. Dogs learn a lot about their humans by doing this. We don't understand a lot of it, but we can look at our humans' eyes and see their sadness or their worry or their "happy." That's our job. That's why the *God of dogs*, the Lord Jesus, the same God who watches over humans, put us here. To be "man's best friend." And we love doing it. Wish I could hug him some time. He doesn't know how much my licks mean to me and how much I want them to help him, just love him, I guess.

We were met soon by Poppy's ol' friend Ron. As I said, he was Poppy's partner on the Tulsa Police Department, and they were really close. I learned that day that a special bond forms between folks who do that policing job, just like the bond that forms between men that had served in combat together. 'Course, Poppy had really close friends, and they all loved each other. He's a good guy, Poppy. He just doesn't realize it sometimes. That's another reason he has me though, to remind him of his goodness.

Anyhow, Poppy and his friends, Ron and Jim, talked into the night telling stories and reviving memories. Jim and I mostly just sat and listened. Late into the droning of human voices, I found myself dozing until I must have slipped soundly into that world of good ol' "doggie dreams," chasing squirrels and sniffing butts and peeing on things.

Suddenly, and with a start, I jerked wide awake and jumped to my feet, the way good dogs will do when they sense danger. There was no danger however. Just a loud retort, during one of their stories.

"Bang," Ron interjected as he was recalling an incident.

The shouted *bang*, I realized, was what triggered my doggie protective instincts.

"The dang gun exploded in the old bastard's hand. I swear, he had just begun to raise it toward me, and it just exploded. Scared the heck out of me and, of course, blew off a couple of his fingers," he continued. Poppy smiling and nodding his head in agreement as if he'd been there and had recalled the incident just as Ron was describing it.

Ron looked at his own hand as if checking to see that all his digits were there, as he said, "I'm not kidding, Godfrey." He continued in a somewhat more subdued tone, "Sometimes I shudder to think how many times the good Lord just stepped in and did something to save our ol' sorry asses."

"Yeah, I know exactly what you mean," Poppy mumbled, more to himself than the rest of us, "and it's hard to find a reason for it. We sure as hell didn't deserve it."

Jim had sat quietly, smiling at times, and laughing at others but mostly listening. Anxious to be involved in the conversation, however, he piped up at this opportune moment, waving an instructional finger for emphasis. "That makes me think…you know how these lawyer commercials on TV always tell you to, 'Come see me. I'll get you what you deserve.'"

He paused a bit, shaking his head, then continued, "Man, I sure as heck hope nobody ever 'gets me what I deserve.'"

A loud laugh, accompanied by several slaps on the knee, endorsed this comment.

"Damn sure got that right, Jim," Poppy responded.

"Amen, brother, don't throw me in that briar patch," Ron offered.

As they all chuckled reflectively, I tried hard to conceive of the "briar patch" analogy, without success. Seemed like a better idea to forget it and try to recapture the squirrel chase.

Another pause ensued as the laughter subsided. Soon Ron continued, still looking at his hand, apparently recalling the sight of the old man's bloodied three-digit bodily extension. "I guess he must have been drinking all day or something. I grabbed his hand and bandaged it best I could, then called for an ambulance. I followed it to Saint Francis and sat with him while I unraveled the rest of the story. He just didn't want to live any longer and couldn't figure out how to end it. Guess he thought I'd do it for him."

"Yeah," Poppy interjected reflectively, "suicide by cop."

"What," Ron responded suddenly, as if jerked out of the grip of a memory that was so powerful, it held him like a vice. "Oh yeah, I know what you're talking about. I just wasn't thinking about the actual terminology. Just never have been able to get that ol' man and the scene out of my mind…sad."

"Sometimes I wake up at the darkest part of the night, and I just get this dread you know," Ron continued, looking at Poppy with that "I know you know what I'm talking about" look on his face, "…

kinda like I'm a character in a really well-made, horror movie, and whatever I'm doing, whatever I'm thinking, wherever I'm going…it just ain't gonna end well, you know."

He paused as the two of them looked away from each other, lost in their own world of thoughts. "And no matter how hard I try, I just can't shake that feeling…and I look over at my wife sleeping soundly, like she doesn't know that bad things are happening all around her… you know."

Now I'd heard Poppy mention that word before, *suicide*, and whenever he said it, it was sorta like he wanted to spit it out of his mouth really quickly so it didn't linger there and 'cause some sorta permanent damaged taste to take root. I kinda thought I knew the feeling, but I wasn't sure. I mean, I'd picked up a few things that I immediately knew were things even dogs ain't supposed to put in their mouths (folks seem to forget sometimes that dogs don't have digits to pick things up with), but somehow, I knew there was another reason he didn't want to linger on this word for very long. Must be something really scary, I guess.

"Graveyard," Poppy responded at length. "Graveyard shift… that's what gets ya into that insomnia shit. Only folks alive at that time are the devils and the cops…and the whole sane world sleeps through it."

"I'll never forget my first suicide," Poppy interjected after a somber reflective pause. "Never forget it. I even recall some of the smells in the house where it happened, cooking odors and a scent of something…I don't know…something that just wasn't supposed to be there and something good people just weren't supposed to have to be exposed to *death*, I guess…maybe *really sad death* or something," he added.

"Poor lady," he continued, "there was a TV dinner half-eaten on the table. You know, one of those dinners people eat by themselves when there's no one to eat with. Looked like she just came home, heated up this TV dinner, ate a couple of bites, then just decided… you know…decided," he continued, telling a story he didn't even want to recall, much less tell someone else, as if he was cursed to have to remember it and tell other folks about it, "decided, you know… decided that it was just too hard, and she couldn't do it anymore."

We all sat there trying to see it, yet trying not to see it, with him. "You know something funny though," he continued, a forced lightness in his voice, as if he was trying to turn this horrible memory into a funny story of sorts, "she put on a really nice dress and pretty shoes…even combed her hair and put light makeup on…then put a rope around her neck and kicked over the stool she was standing on."

We winced when he said that as if we were watching it. Poppy could always tell a story vividly. I even winced a little myself, though I didn't really understand much of this.

"Her fingernails were dug into the palms of her hands, and blood had trickled slightly down onto the floor beneath them."

"Yep," Ron added, a more instructive tone in his voice, "she did that to keep from reaching up and pulling on the rope, stopping herself from doing it."

"And women will always dress up," he picked up the narrative. "They don't want to be embarrassed…funny ain't it."

I sorta knew what he was saying, but somehow it didn't seem funny. It seemed sad to me. They musta gone through a lot, Poppy and his friend Ron. Maybe that was why he was sad sometimes, I figured.

I didn't really know what they were talking about at the time. Seemed like something about the dark of night triggered this mood. Dogs, of course, can't understand that. Sure, we know that bad things come out in the dark. That's when the things that can eat ya prowl the earth. We dogs know about that, but it doesn't make us worry or scare us or anything. It's just the flip side of a coin, I guess. Besides, I think it's not being able to see very well that does it to 'em. Dogs don't have that problem.

My friend Trump told me once that humans can't see in the dark, and it worries them 'cause they don't know what's coming at 'em. Hell, when I was younger, I thought all creatures could see in the dark as well as I could. Guess that *would* put ya in a bad mood.

The mood Ron and Poppy were in just then, though wasn't necessarily bad, was more like sad bordering on bad, I guess. Either way, I didn't like to see them like this. From the look on Jim's face, he didn't understand it either, and he didn't like it either.

The quiet that ensued for a few long seconds seemed to have been summed up by that one single word, *sad*. It's funny, but dogs don't get sad. They get lazy sometimes, and humans misinterpret that for "sad," but it ain't so. Occasionally, one of our buddies dies, gets hit by a car or something (dogs don't get sad, but they do get *stupid* sometimes, thinking they can bite on to and hold on to a dadgum car going forty miles an hour down the road, but *sad*, nope, we don't do that). We know when that happens, we won't get to see these buddies every day anymore, but we also know that we'll see them in doggie heaven, and it's gonna be a lot more fun there. Something else that's funny is that humans think they are the only living creatures in the world that are blessed or cursed with the knowledge that one day they'll no longer be alive on this earth, but that ain't so either. Dogs know they won't live forever. They just don't sit around whining about it, and they don't see it as the end when one of them die. Nope, we just don't do "sad."

I didn't understand it all. Still don't understand the word *sad* the way humans understand it, but at that time, I was compelled to walk over and lick Poppy's friend, Ron, on the back of his hand. That's all that matters most of the time, a good lick on the hand. There's healing power in *doggie spit*. Dogs do that (licking-our-human thing) all the time, just to change the mood. It works every time.

That day, I got a whole new respect for Poppy and for his friend Ron. I knew Poppy was a good guy; he'd always been good to me even when I was a little puppy and used to pee on his socks when he left them lying around after a morning run. Something about the smell of those sweaty socks just made *peeing on them* seem the appropriate thing to do. But as I said, he was patient with me, and instead of kicking me or even yelling, he would just shake his finger and scold me a little. I got the picture too. Yep, Poppy was, and is, a good guy.

But that morning, I realized he wasn't just a *good guy*. He was a real concerned God-fearing American, and so was his buddy Ron. They really did truly care about people, not just cute little dogs. And the people they cared about even seemed a little like unlikely folks to *care about*. They were "unknowns," people who killed themselves 'cause they didn't think anyone cared about them, and old guys who were so miserable at living but just didn't have the courage to kill themselves and had to try to get someone else to do it for them. Yeah, they cared, and yeah, they were good people. I was proud of Poppy and of his friend Ron.

Ron Moulton, as police officers in Tulsa, him and Poppy watched each other's backs for many a year. I liked him right off.

"Well, hell," Ron said, slapping himself on the knees, startling me into abrupt attention and out of my half-sleeping stage, as I lay lounging on the floor. "Let's take Thomas Dooley out and suit him up to see if he can fly one of our choppers around the city. Always heard it was easy enough for a dog to do it, and Dooley seems to be a really smart dog."

"I don't know," Poppy interjected. "'Reckon the city will frown on a *dog-flown* downed chopper?"

"Couldn't care in the least," Ron replied with a wink and a smile.

I had no idea what they were talking about, but I must admit, I was glad to see them out of the *slump*. 'Course, being a dog, I'd trust Poppy anytime, and today was no exception. Besides, we were seemingly about to have *fun*, and I didn't want anything to get in the way of that. Greatest feeling in the world for a dog is to be walking/riding/running/sleeping alongside his human, and during that time, I had him and Ron and his friend Jim all to myself on our *quest*.

It was a beautiful afternoon as we drove out to the outskirts of Tulsa. I hung my head out the window of Ron's old beat-up Jeep Cherokee barking at the passing cars and wincing now and then when a bug hit my nose (my nose has always been a little tinder).

Ron didn't even seem to care if I rubbed thick globs of white *Great Pyrenees* fur all over his old cloth-covered back seat. 'Course, there was nothing I could do about that, but I had been around a lot of folks (girls mostly) who didn't appreciate it.

The smells of a late afternoon "Tulsa, Oklahoma," were all new to me and I tried hard to absorb, categorize, and store all of them, as any responsible canine would. But hell, there was just too many, and they were all intense and interesting.

Now and then, a kid in the back seat of a passing car, the window rolled down, would stick his head out and wave at me with a big smile. Funny thing, certain boys can talk to dogs. Oh, not in words, of course, but they do have the ability to communicate with us. You don't even have to know them either, but you can spot them when you see them. We call 'em dog whisperers. I saw a couple of them that afternoon passing by and smiling at me, my head hung out the window, ears flapping in the breeze. Told 'em I was going to fly a helicopter around Tulsa, and of course, being good dog whisperers, they didn't seem to even question such a thing. There's a really fine line between us and them, most of the time.

When we finally arrived at the Tulsa Police Helicopter Airport, I jumped out of the back seat, straining at the confining length of the leash I was on. Poppy never had been able to move fast enough to keep up with me. As a result, especially when I was excited to see something, or maybe wanting to catch a scampering squirrel or cat, or I caught a whiff of some irresistible odor or something, I always had to pull him, and as far as that *heel* stuff well, I just never got the hang of that.

I scratched eagerly in the dirt, my front claws digging in for traction, still straining against the confines of the leash. Poppy looked disapprovingly at me.

That's another thing I never understood, why humans don't like their dogs to dig in the dirt. I mean after all, that's why God put dirt here anyhow, so dogs could dig in it. Heck, they should have known that.

I looked back at him once in a while and tried to get the point across to him. "Yeah I know, but you gotta smell this, it's better than anything you've ever smelled."

Just a difference of opinion, or I guess desired direction or something. When I was a puppy, I thought my name was, *wait a minute, dammit.* I like *Tom Dooley* much better.

As I strained to get closer to the big round building we seemed to be approaching, anxious to get a look at the thing I was supposed to "fly around Tulsa," I suddenly realized that I didn't even know what it was or what it was supposed to look like, or for that matter, whether I even wanted to *fly* it.

"Wait just a minute," Ron said as we strolled toward the building, me pulling with all my strength. "Dooley can't fly that thing without the right gear."

With that, having captured my attention, he grabbed a black bag that seemed to have been neglected in the corner for some time from the dust covering it and pulled out an ol' leather hat and some big round glasses that looked like the ones ol' man Graves, down the street back home, wears when he's telling the neighborhood kids about the *big war.* He pulled them tight down over my head and tied a long flowing scarf around my neck.

As I looked back at Poppy bewildered, he laughed out loud. I felt kinda humiliated, but dogs get used to that with some of the things their humans put on 'em and make them wear, especially around Christmas. That snooty ol' "Amazing Grace," the poodle down the street, has to wear something that looks like kids' pajamas every Christmas, and her human makes her wear them around the neighborhood so we can all see her. I get so tickled to see her turn red with embarrassment when the guys roll around on the ground laughing and barking at her.

I didn't mind it at the time though. Besides, it was a pleasant change of mood from before, and I was happy to see Ron and Poppy smiling again, and every dog loves it when their humans pay close attention to them, even if they are being humiliated.

"Heck, he's ready to take this puppy up," Ron said, pointing toward me with a declarative thumb slung in my direction.

I looked around for the "puppy" he was talking about. If there was a puppy in the vicinity, I'd ordinarily smell it. We dogs have a really strong odor when we're puppies. Just about that time, Ron grabbed my leash and pulled me toward the door of this really strange contraption they called a helicopter. Now I'd like to describe this *helicopter* to you, my readers, but to tell you the truth, I don't even know where to start. About the best I can say is that it *did* have a door, and Ron was urging me to jump up a bit (since it was off the floor a couple of feet) to get in it.

As luck would have it though, about that time, Ron said, "Okay, Tom Dooley, you passed the test. You were willing to take her up, but maybe we better just let you off the hook on this one. Not a doubt in my mind that you'd have made one heck of a pilot though."

For some reason, I felt a little bit of a relief. Dogs are usually willing to try anything, and me being the *Great Pyrenees* that I am, I surely wouldn't have shied away from it. Be that as it may, I was just as happy to go back to sniffing butts and peeing on stuff. Not sure how my flying career would have faired. I did like the outfit though. Wish Trump coulda seen me.

Houston, we've got a problem, but damn, I
looked good in my Red Baron outfit.

Westward in Search of America

Now dogs understand the concept of sons taking after their
fathers. After all, our sons even look just like us most of the time.
I had twelve brothers and two sisters, and I couldn't even tell them
apart when we were newborn. The sons of our humans don't necessarily look like their fathers, but they do act like them. We can see
that better than most humans can.

So when Ron talked to Poppy about his son, Matt, just sorta updating him a little since Poppy had last seen him (Matt) when he was a baby (Poppy hadn't seen Matt in years), Poppy seemed to understand perfectly. Since Matt had grown to be a man, he had apparently turned out to be just the same sorta man his father was. Matt had become a real true American patriot, just like those we'd set out on our quest to find.

"Yeah, Godfrey," Ron said, a proud smile on his face, "Matt is a real supporter of the freedoms we always fought for, especially the second amendment…even runs his own shooting range and pistol shop. You gotta stop to see him on your way west."

Now, I didn't know what a *second amendment* was, but I did know what a gun was. It was *loud and scary*. All dogs knew that. I could even remember the smell of gunpowder from a trip I went on with Poppy and his friend Jim, who was a hunter and had a couple of bird dogs (funny, they didn't look like birds to me, but maybe I wasn't thinking about them in the way I should). The smell was sorta bitter to me, like old dog food and wasn't nearly as clear as another dog's butt, but humans, especially human hunters, seemed to get really excited when it was in the air. Poppy wasn't a hunter, but most of his friends were. He just didn't like the idea of killing anything.

"Nothing 'cept other humans," he'd often say, "especially when they feel the same way about you. No sense in killing anything else though, as long as you can go to the grocery store and buy a can of beans."

I realized once again that the smell of gunpowder was connected to the loud sound, and all of it came from the guns humans were so proud of. My two "bird" dog friends got really excited about it when it was in the air too. Maybe they just turned into birds when the excitement would get *exciting enough*.

I also didn't know this *second amendment* thing had to have a *supporter*, but from the conversation, I gathered there was a connection there somewhere. I also came to a clear understanding that the guns, the second amendment, and being a real American conservative, were all connected in a strong way.

"You gotta stop and see Matt on your way west, Godfrey," Ron continued. "He'd really love to see ya, and I can pretty well guarantee you that you'll see some true Americans out there hanging out and shooting at his range."

"Wouldn't miss it," Poppy answered. And with that, we loaded up on our *home on wheels*. I ran to my favorite window, hung my head out, and barked a few times just to say goodbye to Ron, and we rolled slowly out of the parking lot heading west.

There was a renewed smell of optimism and excitement in the air, and I just couldn't stop soaking it up and barking in return. Soon, we'd turned onto a wider road, picked up speed, and my ears began flapping appropriately in the cool morning Oklahoma breeze.

Outside Tulsa, we drove for a couple of hours west on a road that was so straight and uneventful, it seemed like we never moved. The scenery was as *western*, two hours in, as it was in the first five minutes of driving.

Nothing seemed to change, other than the color of the cows grazing contentedly in the fields. The flimsy barbed wire fences separating them from the busy highway traffic seemed almost an afterthought. It was obvious, the barriers they created were more of a gentlemen/cow agreement than a true hindrance to movement. Some of the fence poles, made from crooked rotted tree branches, seemed to struggle just to remain upright.

I even thought of barking a word or two of encouragement to them, to escape their confines, until the thought occurred to me that maybe they were completely satisfied with where they were, that maybe the fences were there just to give them an excuse to refrain from wandering. Maybe they could graze contently, feeling no assault on their pride of animal independence by declaring to themselves, "We have to remain on these grounds. The fences dictate such."

I snapped occasionally at the strange smells that wafted by my nose as I hung my head out the window. Dogs just do that. It's not like we're trying to catch something, I don't think. It's just *what we do*, sorta like chasing the ice cream truck. Of course, we know we wouldn't know what to do if we ever caught it. Besides, its only fun if it's trying to get away from you. It's sorta like a baby reaching out to try to catch a bunch of fireworks exploding in the sky in brilliant flashes of unbelievable colors and brightness, simply wanting to hold them in its little hands, and own them for a minute. So that's why we chase the ice cream truck, I guess.

Suddenly, I realized that I was wasting much, too much valuable *strange odor* sniffing time, musing on such irrelevancy, as the enclosure of cows and such. Life was short, and there were far too may smells left unsniffed to waste time contemplating the trivial.

With just such a thought in mind, I returned to sniffing vigorously, barking irritatingly, and wagging my fluffy white tail much too strenuously, shedding fine tufts of white hair throughout the confines of the motor coach, each catching a ride on a breeze, intent on finding a resting place in the coffee cups of Poppy and his friend, Jim.

Soon we took a couple of turns down roads that all seemed the same, dusty and so straight, they disappeared into the horizon rather than curving into obscurity. Finally, we slipped off the road into a gravel parking lot that was filled with pickup trucks and jeeps, most with a gun rack in the rear window. Poppy opened the door, grabbed my Mississippi State University dog leash, and we jumped to the ground stretching our legs and yawning.

The *pop, pop* of gun shots came from somewhere in the rear of the building behind a metal fence. I didn't need an explanation as to the origin. I knew from my hunting dog buddies that folks were shooting at something nearby.

I had heard the sounds of hunting gun shots in the past, and I knew that they were few and spread out over a longer time. These shots were *many* and close together. These shots were just for fun.

In the distance, I heard a lone bark of protestation, most likely from a dog who was trying to sleep. I barked a couple of sympathetic replies as if to say, "I hear ya. You should hear it from this close."

Just then, the front door of a small nondescript metal building opened, and a young man came running out with a smile of welcome on his face. I felt strangely at home from the sight of his face. He seemed truly glad that we had arrived.

Matt Moulton, son of Poppy's ol' police partner,
standing in front of his shooting range.

"Hey, Uncle Godfrey," the young man shouted at Poppy, waving his hands in the air enthusiastically. "Man, it's been a long time."

"Matthew," Poppy replied as he threw his arms around the young man's neck. "I would have recognized you anywhere. You look just like your ol' man. I haven't seen you in years, and I would still have recognized you."

"The last time I saw this kid, he just barely reached my knees in height," Poppy said to Jim. "I guess I've known him since he was a baby."

"We were just talking to your dad this morning," he continued, not waiting for a reply from Jim.

"I know," Matt replied smiling. "He called me and told me you were coming."

I had long realized that humans had a standard routine of greetings, and each one was specifically tailored to the situation. The only thing left to add to the words was the accompanying facial expressions. I had learned over the years to recognize the level of interest in the relationship from Poppy's facial expressions. I knew, for instance, when he ran across someone he'd just as soon not bumped into, from the facial contortions and smiles, or lack thereof.

Dogs, on the other hand, knew whether they were welcomed long before the first bark. We can sniff the air preceding the approach of a fellow canine, from a distance of a hundred yards, and tell what type of greeting to expect. Saves a lot of time.

There was no doubt Poppy was happy about this meeting.

"Come on in." Matt motioned toward the small metal building. "I want to show you my business."

We walked in to the building, no one objecting to having a dog inside. I was always instantly connected to any business or home that seemed to welcome dogs. 'Course, I am an exceptionally good-looking, well-mannered dog, so I was used to folks welcoming me, but when one of my "less attractive" brothers was welcomed "inside," it showed the owners of the establishment in question were unusually attuned to the finer things of life. Few people are acutely aware that dogs "inside" are really good luck to all present. And the *doggier* the smell, the more luck the canine brings. Folks just aren't aware of that, I suppose.

The inside of Matt's business was bustling with people, mostly men, but a few women. All were enthusiastically discussing their shooting expertise or the latest guns and related shooting equipment.

Of course, they all stopped to comment on the *beautiful animal in their midst* (I say that with all humility, but it is a fact. Such comments are common when I am present). Once these comments subsided, a few folks, mostly the women in the bunch, *ooohed* and *awwwhed* while rubbing my ears but all returned to the subject of guns and their purposes and the best guns for their personal objectives.

"Tell you the truth," one portly older gentleman wearing a sweater and a ball cap that seemed to represent a military unit he was affiliated with, opined, "the reason people with a gun are victimized by bad folks, even though they are standing there, *gun in hand*, is because they hesitate."

"The reason people hesitate, especially women"—he glanced furtively around the area and emphasized, somewhat reluctantly, with an obviously arthritically-impaired index finger—"is because even if they are in fear of their lives, deep down, no one, especially women, wants to kill somebody."

"Bad guys," he continued, eyes narrowed, eyebrows raised instructively, "recognize this. They can sense that hesitation, and a second is all they need to snatch away a gun or jump a weaker victim."

"That's why folks should always keep that short-barreled Judge revolver close by, loaded with 410-gauge birdshot rounds."

"You see," he continued, following a short pause for emphasis, "when you're armed with a weapon that isn't going to kill anyone, unless its pointed right at their head, you're not likely to have that subconscious fear of taking a person's life."

"You can just point it at their balls"—he chuckled audibly—"and blast away, secure in the knowledge that you ain't gonna kill anybody. Hell, the most you're going to do is end a man's *procreative career*." He laughed uproariously. "The bad guy, on the other hand, will realize there'll be no hesitation on your part, right off the bat, and he'll be the one hesitating as he tries to decide whether he wants to risk such a loss by attempting to get the jump on you. That's a gamble few men are willing to take."

"For that reason," he resumed the narration in summation, "I'd recommend keeping that little ol' equalizer, *the Judge*, close at hand for self-defense."

Various related conversations and nods of agreement could be seen and heard around the spacious display area, and everyone seemed to be at ease among like-minded Americans.

"My customers like coming here and just hanging out." Matt looked at Poppy, with an obvious sense of pride in his establishment. "There's nothing more *American and God-fearing* than relishing in the knowledge that our nation gives everyone the right to 'stand his ground' and not give in to fear and intimidation from those who are stronger or meaner or just intent on taking what is yours, just because they want it."

I somehow sensed from this conversation that we had found a handful of folks who fit the bill and satisfied our quest, though I knew Poppy and his friend Jim were going to want to keep looking.

In the near distance, loud popping sounds could be heard. While I would normally have hidden my nose under something tight and comforting, the way us dogs tend to do, somehow, I knew the sounds weren't threatening.

"I just feel like I'm 'doing my part,' Godfrey," Matt said. "This is what America is."

"I know your dad is proud of you, Matt," Poppy replied. "It sort of reminds me of the sounds and smells from the ol' firing range days when him and I were on the department."

"You know," he continued, his eyes gazing off at a memory rather than an object, "I used to hate that range 'cause I was always a bad shot. My heart wasn't in it, though I knew how important it was."

Suddenly, he laughed out loud when his memory struck something pleasant and funny. "You know, I just remembered, if we didn't score a certain minimum score, we had to stay late and go through the whole damn thing again. Your dad was always a better shot than me, so he'd shoot a target right next to mine."

"Well"—he paused and pointed an instructive finger—"knowing I'd probably fail the minimum, he'd fire the necessary rounds in his target to qualify, then aim slightly off to the right, and fire the remaining rounds into my target so I wouldn't have to stay late."

He paused again. Then, in summation, he said, "We always had a party to go to somewhere right after the range, and your dad didn't want me to be delayed."

Westward We Go

For the next few days, we continued west toward California. The days were a maze of short trips down interesting dirt roads, stops at Dew Drop Inns for a hamburger ("Now that's a real hamburger," Poppy and Jim would say over and over again.), and *out of the way* motor coach and trailer campgrounds. At these locations, we met "the real Americans," and Poppy and Jim seemed more and more encouraged as we talked to these folks.

'Course, everyone knows that dogs have superhuman (actually, superdog) hearing. As we would walk away from conversations with the folks we'd met, I'd often heard whispers of, "What are they doing, and why are they asking us all these questions?" or maybe, "Where are they from or what do you s'pose they want…heck, they may be fishermen for God or something." Got these comments mostly from campgrounds in towns with plenty of churches.

Most often, however, I'd hear the longing wispy comments, "Wonder where they're going from here…wish I could go."

As one day slipped into the next, each bringing with it wondrous strange new smells and sounds and the brightest stars I'd ever seen at night, Poppy and I both began to feel that "tug of home." I couldn't help wondering what my friends Amazing Grace and Snot-a-Lot and, of course, my best friend, Trump were all up to and if they missed me.

Poppy was more and more becoming preoccupied with the love of his life, and my doctor, Dr. Lena Jo. I could tell it was becoming harder and harder on him. Even dogs worry that they're going to be forgotten by their loved ones when they aren't around, and I guess, the older we all get, the more acutely we feel those things.

Yep, it was time to wrap this journey up and head home. Before we did, however, we had time to meet a few other real *God-loving America-loving* friends like.

Christy, from Amarillo. God sure does make *pretty girls* out west.

Police officers Earnie and Audria from LA, California.

Members of the Northern California Firefighters.
Risking their lives for the America they love.

Poppy, Jim, and me. Not sure of the significance,
but Poppy declared, "'Nuff said."

And all the while, we were reminded that no matter how many mistakes us Americans (dogs and humans) make as we try to become better people and walk in the path God has provided for us, we still live in a land our fathers bequeathed to us, a land that is the ultimate destination for people the world over. As we drove down the road in El Paso, Texas, the Mexican border in sight, Poppy rubbed my head and said, "I can't imagine what we must look like to all those people, how we must really seem 'that bright shiny city on the hill' to them."

"You know what," Jim offered, "that's exactly what we are. That's why we tear up when 'The Star-Spangled Banner' is played and sung."

"Yep," he continued as I hung my head out the window in the predawn darkness, soaking in the smells and aromas from two separate nations that swirled and intertwined in the air, combining to make one glorious signature scent, declaring a love of God and a love of life, "the greatest country in the world, and she's all ours."

The predawn thin line separating two nations in El Paso, Texas.

Prologue

On the way home, driving down Interstate 20 east between Shreveport, Louisiana, and the state line at Vicksburg, Mississippi, I had the pleasure of listening to Poppy and his friend Jim sorta sum up the trip. They were both tired and both looking forward to getting home, but they seemed truly anxious to sum up a successful adventure. They really wanted to be able to establish that *God-fearing America-lovin'* America was out there and alive and well, and that they'd found it.

'Course, I was the one who had to write this book, so naturally I wanted to see the "so what" aspect of it more than either of them.

The closer we got to home, the more energized and excited we got. Poppy and I had traveled together all over the country, and we were always excited to see new things in the mountains or plains or be close to the oceans, but there was just something really special about getting back home. I could smell Mississippi in the air. 'Course, that wasn't any big deal 'cause dogs can smell everything. But this was different. Even Poppy could smell this. As we'd get closer after a long trip, he'd always turn to me and say, "Smell that, Mr. Dooley (he always called me something silly like *Mr. Dooley* when he was happy), that's 'Misippi' in the air."

He always said it like that too, *Misippi*. It's always good to have a home base, like a strong rock to tie your string to. Then you could leave if you wanted to, and all you had to do when you were tired of the road and wanted to go home was just follow your string back to the rock it was tied to.

It occurred to me right about that time that my *doggie God* was like that too. As long as I kept my string tied to him, I could always find my way back home and to him, if I got lost. Now both his and

47

my/our home were close enough to sniff in the air, and I could actually see them. 'Course, Poppy always said that God was always there, but I tied my string anyhow, you know, just in case.

It also struck me that Poppy had another reason for being anxious and in a hurry to get home—his sweetheart, Dr. Lena Jo. Everything was there, just a short drive away, and we were really excited about it. I couldn't wait to tell Trump and ol' Snot-a-Lot and prissy Amazing Grace. Each time Poppy and me would leave on a trip and get back home, after the perfunctory butt sniffing had been completed, me and the whole gang would sit around and talk and bark at each other for hours and hours. When I told a really funny story of the road, ol' Snot-a-Lot would roll around on the ground barking and slinging crap all over everybody, from that drooling mouth and nose of his. Man, I couldn't wait to see the guys and especially my best friend, Trump.

Heck, I remember once, Poppy and I were driving way out in the prairie in Wyoming or somewhere (can't remember exactly), and we came upon this farm that had these big birds (biggest birds I ever saw in my life), and Poppy told me that sometimes they actually stuck their whole heads down in the ground like they were looking around for worms or something. Well, I could understand him maybe stretching the truth once in a while, and I was just about to snort my disapproval of this whopper, but all of a sudden, one of them actually did just that, stuck his head right down in the ground. I swear it, I saw it with my own eyes. When I got back home from that trip and told the guys, they just barked and barked and ran around trying to stick their heads down in the ground in any holes they could find. I was sure ol' Snot-a-Lot was gonna get his big ol' *bulldog* head stuck somewhere. Trump, being the smartest of us all, just sat there looking at them and shaking his head in amusement.

"Well, whatdayathink, Mr. Dooley," he said while he rubbed the top of my head so vigorously, I thought he'd pull some of my favorite white fluff loose. "Did we find it or not? Did we find the 'God-fearing America' we were looking for?" Following a short pause, he continued with a big grin. "I think so. Yep, I truly think so."

He was talking to both me and Jim at the time, but it was a rhetorical question anyhow (*Rhetorical*, what a word, and me, just a dog. Heck, I couldn't wait to get at that pen and paper. Got this in the bag.). He knew as well as we did that it was there, and that we had found it.

I never wasted a lot of time wishing I could actually talk. Dogs can communicate pretty well without the convenience of the actual words, but for some reason right then, I wanted to say, "Heck yeah, we did. Sure, we did, and you know what…I told you we would. Me, Tom Dooley. Yep, I told you we would."

About the Author

D r. Godfrey Garner is a veteran Special Forces Counterintelligence US Army veteran. He served two military tours and six civilian government-related tours in Afghanistan in intelligence and counterintelligence. He is the author of *Danny Kane and the Hunt for Mullah Omar, Clothed in White Raiment,* and *The Balance of Exodus* and coauthor of Taylor & Francis published textbooks, *Intelligence Analysis Fundamentals* and *Origins of Terrorism: The Rise of the World's Most Formidable Terrorist Groups.* He is a permanent faculty member at Mississippi College and an adjunct professor at Tulane University on the Mississippi Gulf Coast, teaching intelligence analysis and counterterrorism for Homeland Security. He is, additionally, a PhD dissertation committee member at Belhaven University. He is the author of more than forty articles for *Homeland Security Today,* journal of *American Diplomacy* and journal of *Foreign Affairs.*